CASEY'S COMPOST

Written & Illustrated by Bonnie Bright

Casey, in loose fitting hand-me-down pants,
Was waiting for Mom while playing with ants.
Soon, they would leave to visit Miss Bunny,
With a basket of jars, to fill with her honey.

Miss Bunny's house was a mile out of town,
Nestled in hills that go up and then down.
Away from the smog, near a fresh running stream,
Surrounded by trees and farms full of green.

When the car sputtered up to her organic farm,
Miss Bunny appeared; chickens under each arm.
Casey leapt from the car, ran towards her to see,
His two favorite chickens, McPuff and Dundee.

Miss Bunny smiled, surrounded by bees,
"C'mon, let's spread compost under my trees."
They then walked together past old Mr. Wert,
Until finally they reached a box full of dirt.

"Compost," said Bunny, "Feeds plants with my trash.
I collect it all here in my private stash.
Made up of stale food, leaves, paper and poop.
You can make it from junk mail and bowls of old soup."

"It's loaded with bugs that break it all down
To a nutritious soil that is rich and dark brown.
I feed it to all of the plants on my farm.
And, as you can see, it works like a charm."

The rest of the day, they shovelled and spread,
'Til all of the fruit trees were happily fed.
McPuff and Dundee ate all of the bugs.
Mom had her honey and Casey had slugs.

Thanking Miss Bunny, they jumped in the car.

Casey decided to wish on a star.

Watching the land, turn from green into grey,

He wished Bunny's compost would come save the day.

He thought and he thought about what he could do.
Maybe, just maybe, he could compost too.
"Mom, can I compost?" He said with wide eyes.
But she looked at him and to his surprise,
His mom said, "No there's too many bugs.
They'll creep in the house and crawl on my rugs."

That night, after dinner, he thought to himself,
Why not take that box from up on the shelf?
I'll start my own compost right under my bed.
He stuffed his pant pockets with noodles and bread.

Each meal, Casey scraped up the leftover food.
Then added old leaves and apples half chewed.
And just when he felt really proud of himself,
His mom found the laundry and let out a yelp!

"Casey! Come here, I must talk to you!
What's wrong with your pockets, they're covered in goo?!"
She told him to stop, so the next day at school,
He made a new plan that was totally cool...

As students lined up at the trash each day,
Casey opened his bag and collected away.
As time went by, he built up his pile.
Kids thought he was weird, but gave him a smile.
They tossed their old food right into his pack,
Then they walked away laughing behind his back.

He piled his collection, beneath a dead bush,
But then, he got caught by Principal Tush.

"To the office, young man. I just called your mom.
You'll need to explain what's been going on."

"Mom," exclaimed Casey, "please don't glare at me.
I was trying to compost. Look there and you'll see?"

Outside the window was a bush full of green,
Surrounded by dead ones, it looked like a queen.
Casey's mom smiled and explained in great haste,
"He's feeding the plants and reducing your waste."

A few weeks went by. It was back-to-school night.
And up on the stage, to Casey's delight,
Were Principal Tush and Mayor O'Toole,
Announcing a program called Compost Your School.

They said, "Thank you Casey," and started to clap.
"The school will add bins to collect our food scraps."
A composting program soon spread through the town,
And soon things began to turn green all around.

Several months later while out riding bikes,
Casey and Mom saw something they liked.
The town now looked better than ever before,
With green sprouting up outside every front door.

Start here &
follow clockwise...

+

50% Water,
(like a damp sponge)

+

Air=sticks create
open spaces

+

Microbes form
naturally

+

Humans add, mix
and maintain

=

The pile
generates heat.

&

Carbon dioxide
is created.

&

Water vaporizes
as the pile heats

&

Compost!
Add it to your soil.
Plants love it!

What's happening inside your compost pile?

A compost pile has gazillions of microbes (organisms so small they can't be seen without a microscope). They feast on organic materials, converting them to compost.

Like us, microbes work most efficiently with a proper diet, in specific temperature ranges, and adequate oxygen levels.

What can I compost?

Food Scraps...

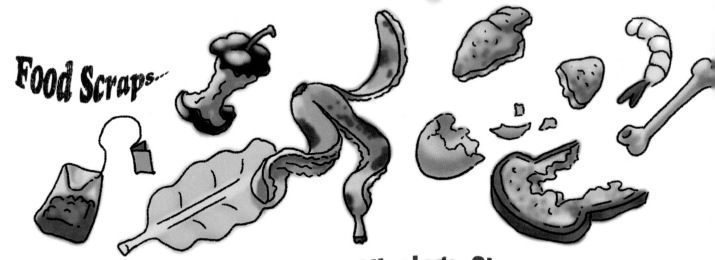

Leaves, Wood Shavings, Grass Clippings, Straw...

Paper Products...

Want to heat things up?

Add manure from cows, chickens, horses, goats to heat things up in your compost pile and help it cook. A great instructional book on composting is "The Humanure Handbook", written by Joseph Jenkins. This book provides information and guidelines on composting, over flowing landfills, ground water contamination, rey-water systems, plant filtration...

I hope you have found this book helpful and inspiring. You may also like "Joe's New Windrows, Reduce, Reuse, Recycle". If you have suggestions, I'm always looking to improve the usefulness of this book, and the other books I have created.

You can reach me via my web site at www.brightillustration.com. I appreciate your review!

What are some of the things I can do, and have done, to help the planet?

AT HOME
- Compost
- Grow fruits and vegetables in the back yard
- Bake bread using a bread machine (no plastic bread bags!)
- Cook in a solar oven outside (mine is store-bought, but you can make your own!)
- Solar panels on the roof
- Pick up trash around the neighborhood and the lake
- I fenced the back yard using fence posts I found floating in the lake
- I built a raised planter bed and a set of stairs using wood I found floating in the lake
- Paperless billing
- Use a washable, reusable hanky instead of facial tissue
- Use washable, cloth napkins instead of paper towels
- Clean with vinegar, water, baking soda
- Bamboo toothbrush
- Laundry soap strips that come in a paper envelope (no plastic!)
- Raise ducks or chickens for eggs and compost the manure
- Gravity fed drinking water filtration system

SHOPPING
- Look for boxed water or water in aluminum cans
- Select organic produce
- Choose paper egg cartons over plastic or Styrofoam
- Put loose fruits and vegetables in your own bags
- Paper milk and juice cartons
- Buy used clothing
- Bring reusable cloth bags to the store
- Look for food products available in compostable plastic, like Sunrays

EATING OUT
- Bring your own Tupperware for leftovers
- Refuse those Styrofoam to-go cups and containers
- Use your own mug at the coffee shop

TRANSPORTATION
- Carpool or ride on a bus or a train
- Ride a bike or walk
- Save up for an electric vehicle

Thank you!

Made in the USA
Las Vegas, NV
11 November 2023